DYSSEMIA SLEAZE

Adeena Karasick

Talonbooks
2000

Talonbooks
#104—3100 Production Way
Burnaby, British Columbia, Canada V5A 4R4

Printed and bound in Canada by Hignell Printing Ltd.

First Printing: April 2000

Talonbooks are distributed in Canada by General Distribution Services,
325 Humber College Blvd., Toronto, Ontario, Canada M9W 7C3
Tel.:(416) 213-1919; Fax:(416) 213-1917.

Talonbooks are distributed in the U.S.A. by General Distribution Services Inc.,
4500 Witmer Industrial Estates, Niagara Falls, New York, U.S.A. 14305-1386
Tel.:1-800-805-1083; Fax:1-800-481-6207.

Canadä

The publisher gratefully acknowledges the financial support of the Canada Council
for the Arts; the Government of Canada through the Book Publishing Industry
Development Program; and the Province of British Columbia through the British
Columbia Arts Council for our publishing activities.

Canadian Cataloguing in Publication Data

Karasick, Adeena, 1965-
  Dyssemia sleaze

  Poems.
  ISBN 0-88922-434-X

  I. Title.
1.A74D97 2000   C811'.54   C00-910364-3
PR9199.3.K365D97 2000

ACKNOWLEDGEMENTS

With thanks to the editors who published earlier versions or parts of this work: Jena Osman and Juliana Spahr at *Chain*; Clarise Foster and Janine Tschuncky at *CV2*; Deborah Greniman at *Nashim: A Journal of Jewish Womens' Studies and Gender Issues*; Tamara Fairchild at *Canadian Journal of Contemporary Literary Stuff*; Lindsay Tipping at *in.grave ink*; R. W. Megans at *Kairos 11*; Joe Blades at *New Muse of Contempt*; Jacques Debrot at *9-0*; jennifer LoveGrove at *dig.— a journal of poetry, etc,*. Derek Beaulieu at *Filling Station*; bill bissett and Ryan Knighton at the *Capilano Review*; Gary Sullivan and Nada Gordon at *Read Me* (*www.jps.net/nada*); Heather Haley and Carol Hamshaw at the *Edgewise Electrolit Centre* (*www.edgewisecafe.org*); Jennifer Ley at *Perihelion* (*webdelsol.com/Perhelion*); David Dowker at the *Alterran Poetry Assemblage* (*home.ican.net*); Ethan Paquin at *Slope* (*www.slope.org*); Naomi Savage at the University of Toronto English Library (*www.library.utoronto.ca/canpoetry*) and Sandie Drzewiecki at the League of Canadian Poets (*www.poets.ca*). Renditions of many of these poems appear in the film, "Women I Know" (special thanks to producer Pauline Urquhart).

In addition i would like to thank the Canada Council, Foreign Affairs, UNDP, Sharon Nelson and Karl and Christy Siegler for their meticulous editing, incredible generosity, and ongoing support and dedication to my work.

*The limits of my language
mean the limits of my world
(Wittgenstein)*

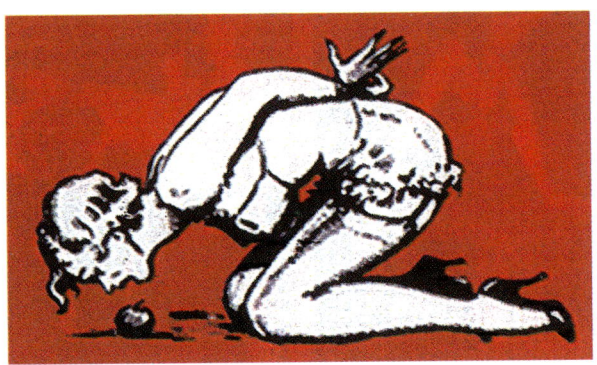

...as i trace without trace this inviolable
secret without depth. without place. without name.
without destination, hyperbolytic in excessive
measure without measure and without return. In
the chiasmatic invagination of all anamnestic
confrontation. without lysis. without nexum.
without desmos and stricture.
in the invisible asylum of....

For
Sean &
Safia Fiera

& to these letters which t/ravel together,
mysteriously united, one stretched towards
the other, one emerging from the other's side, one
suckling the other; folding in on these letters i belong to
that carry me and dance both within the pages
of this text and as social, historical
effects of reference.

And this is the letter that will not leave. That i cannot write. This is the letter. The letter that falls in its carrying. In the killing of its crushing, its clinging in its excesses and its masks. This is the letter which lifts up and travels from one word to another grimaces in the torment of its hardening. In its emptiness. In its own contamination. This is the letter buried without madness. Drowning in its own inexplicable cry. And this is the letter, the interletter that does not write. Does not speak but in nightmares. In the death of its enunciation which rises, swells in indefatiguable profusion. Renders its presence in immediacy and madness. In hysterical desire. This letter of letters of doors, thresholds, capacities, amplitudes, omissions and promises. Depths and pleasures. That trembles with tension. Stretched / in its torments of glyphs, glas gloss / glassary rasp lisps in its missing. In its hiddeness and limits. In scattered separations mocks in anxiety. In foreignness and deception swells into the letter this letter sung in its horror, anger, agon. Suffers in substitution, redistribution and bears the unbearable, irrepressibly posited in staggered familiarity, in hunger and withdrawal, dissolute desire; the letter of the letter that witnesses and withstands its usage.

Mehaneh Yehuda

Body against body. In a
complex process of struggle, bodies
united in the clutch of separation (Hélène Cixous)

I

Yon fisticuffs.
Coughs as picante come stalkery flocks
in an apophantic calico addict

flounced with fretted foaming
as hunger floats in cadenced drapes spun pungent
primped in plush proxy.

In the outré angst
of persnickety picolo olé —
In the eager longing of
inadequacy scats. Without scandal or
song. Or certainty sought

in the saying and the sd so / up-sized as
ancillary seizes

And as bodies flung flourish
in the familiar poisoning of
what's witnessed —

call me *lucky, lucky, lucky*

& don't bother me with your
calêche attaché briôche caché.

in the minutia of
my binding. The
text of yr vexed nexum

integument augment grog
haptic slack scars

And, as irreducible tension wells
in the politics of a promise

surrenders without horror
without words like an extrinsical rinse
encrusting in separation. devoured
by this hunger gnawing

In excoriated sorrow.
In the agony of abandon.

- *HAMAS*, literally an acronym for the *Harakat al-Muqawama al-Islamiya* (the Islamic Resistance Movement) and literally denotes "zeal" or "enthusiasm". The *HAMAS* Covenant, however, interprets its name to mean "strength and bravery". My Hebrew-English dictionary defines the Hebrew word *hamas* (*het-mem-samech*) as: To Displace. Rob. Destroy. Corruption. Violence.

So, don't fritter yr flapjacks
in a frugal gulag gumption.

In a fracked up / uppity sup

      synapse a go-go

Put yr moment where yr mouth is

In the insouciance of the intractable
or the insipient slip of a sassy-ass
sashay / satchel câchet kiss
câisse causal

pungent flap fractal

or in the faux suave swivel of
yr tizzy.

And, take yr paratactic prophylactic in a
ventriloquy se crée

And grind yr

Haughty tauty tater-tot.

in the calm torment of
uninhabitable anguish gripped
by all that is elliptical
rested in this jagged odour
of wetted breeks, rotting fits irrupts / in abhorrence triumphs
between measures, monsters, mutants, moreover

So, behold the hidden had huddles.

Without *sic* succulence or succor,

in this massacre fiacre
mishap shapen E sharp sherpa or
shrapnel act.

And, take yr boondocker clodhopper wafflestomper

In persecuted immanence
In the proximity of annoyance

Across fields. Across flesh.
And yr furnished adjunct

gorged in the horror of yr
messy fesnyng.

Mehaneh Yehuda II

And, in intolerable hunger,
her ripple tress poise

thrusts in the forage of yr
tee-hee hoopla. Her throaty porous wrenched in its nodding
streams in the beaten dusk shoulders
of her merging flurry misplaced in its clinging,
in its shudders in its manic slam requiem
chafes in her

skid squat
salsa sucker spunk

In a vocabulary constabulary.
In the simulation of the cumulous.

*

So, sweep a deep trickle / in this anti-verismilitude bathos,

for, *who* echoes across
her coming carpeted

13

in elegua longing as bygone beginnings beleaguered legacies
beckon. In the refuse fissure fitted. In the wherefrom frolic
frocks as focus fetish clings.
Foretold in a fading, fastened in

the nausea of ipseity illeity,
a minaret arrêt or minuet peut-être

*

Yet, as indignant ditto splits,
my interregnum nestled in her limn fuzz glut trough skitter
graft ganglia
like a syllabic ab havoc cicadic claque
wrenched in pursed slur streams
in lissome drifts // as her tongue scales // throbs as
tossed whispers. calyx vespers vaunt musky hem twines
gropes breathless as this limit unfolds in blunt gathers. In
spectral tides and reticent edges, like the ache
of lexicon curls. In
feral fluke skiffs, cirrus quill callings
and clearly.

*

But, bruised rust ochre chills in
mad facets. Sculpted in scattered curves
as breath fells wrung with stuffed tufts. With
silica slips tipsy grieving, my
twisted impress flails
in seeping strictures enfolds in her
hunger. In her articulate tongues tucked

in torque wyck ankle ebbs in
serial surfaces like chic smut fluff

                        which prints across

in the grammar of
a glottal broth bother,

((as kissing splice soaks, skims riggish —
slung in straddled debt, bleating
from the griefs of

flung suck slack basking

in zones of ambivalence
as moist haste cramps

in her heaving lapsus,
shattered rasp bough trough hinges
in her harrowing. in luminous shivers
stuttered furies fugue their ravish / wounds
in bitter dissembling / shrieks in their venom
in the crush of gutted swells wrested in lattice tain
silica contours and gathers

in the burning.
in her sodden hubris hyly hung

in the silence // of isosceles sauce of her ipso sotto siting of
her bolistic torque basque

& the *all too* blemished

epidemic emic etic edict [sic]

unduly warped and

ɕɑnɕly ɪn

slim pivot vista squints / in
upsprung sobs of blunt tongue stutters
in gnarled portents and spent dulcets
slip in the slurred urgency of her suave fop fleets
of her plummy terror / sores
like a pixilate syntax in swank circuitries
and cusps her suffer spate unctuous ripped with
russet swallows and frayed trope spasms of rubbing splits
l'anguishing in the insouciance sluice

of this pom pom pomposity,
this flute spume spar of folly.

Mehaneh Yehuda III

So, twitter this:

In a razz spaz frazzle dolop squad quadrant
with no armatures, articulations,
her wobbling abject bunged in an upsurge buffer
branded in its traject dispersed
in thick stem circuitry, in drained linkages

*

And when her blemished settle ravished in a luxuriant flurry,
her giddy influx, a flourish of bloated hope

like sassy squib hinges of secret chapters chisleled
with left hemp shiftings, with

desuetude
suave étude

in a bitter billow flout tout tatter flank flailing folly lisp
wisp fister wafter fop.

*

And, as *ab* intra *autre* outrance enters
as tough fluff —

this promise congeals in loose syntax, in turbulent blockages
and fixed torque totic tainted taunts

radically ambiguated

in the vexed text trim, the slapstick scription
of her inexpressible instants dipped

in a viscera pith
purge splurge proxy

*

But, as yearning shuttles in
the exult injury, in the wad of
false context her liaison strays
in the palimpsest of her teeming / in
the grammar of secret swoons, swoop spur swivels —
And, in lieu of her scruple looplet, her
circuli alibi clots in
bloused slippage
wigged out in furtive
fault sauce
fritters / her body
weaves

     spatially tendered
     with tongue tulle tallies

               (and variant glosses).

which broods through her sissy fit
      surfaces rutted
            in fluttered fancies.

In flattened referents

          sweating in

florid ditto licks /
a lexicon of
zip quilts quarried in
her longing
body squeals like
rubbable melba or a mueble labial
slain in waxen flax flushes.

And, as normative tilts ooze in a choreography of tropic
blot clotters
a cotillion of many cullers, isolata eros swigs in
blunt pulses & skins the surface of
her dimpled limits
fermented in riggish gashings
grasped in spronged frottage ruffled fetchings
fraught with hâute conduits.

Improbable Grammars IV

Metamorphosis of
la langue de la momie

Quelle Sputum or
And say, why dont'cha try it with words?

In a witty "ditty dawn's up," a
glossalallic frothy slop as her hot tongue suck salve

in the clamour of the surplus.
In a lurid body of desire.

So, Tickle me, Almost in a yon dandy
of bobbing obbligati, and sock it to my sestet
as yr dappled appliqué
chronically knotted in flustered ellipsis

For, when all atwitter,
puckered with plump pickin's pasted in the thickness of
eeks scant hâute scum touts
a hard puty gerand errant parted in a foray
foyer o yea.

In the hesitant gait of
her trembling, in the range of

> yr reference / wrenched in the hem
> of the haw. In the hello
> of the hollow

in uvular forego ergo.

As yr moist scat scourges soaking in my
subtext fissures across a tracery of despotic flotsam, a
flotilla of figural limbers, lick my sedition as you drape yr
lilting lexicon around my sassy magma spun gushing and
crammed with the quizzical thrill of sticky particulars
tinged with the sputter of hâute turrets, ruffled strollings as
my mandalay souchsong slips softly

For, when *daylight come an' i wanna go*
where no glib regret garment guarantees

a propaedeutic hermeneutic
in the chaise câisse casque caulked

(with hubris.)

Do you know the way to say

ipseity illeity lay he who

swaddled in a stable labial able
pump gumption sump

So, *hush little baby don't you cry*
mama's gonna bake you
a desquamation pie

and if that hypostasis don't sing
mama's gonna sauté
a codicil docile

in the enigma swig mottled clog of

an excusary ruse
or lucky lucre ludic clues.

So, don't you be cryin' over spilled
lexical sects as
social surrogates surrender in

a dosey doe dulcet
mucilage fuselage
silica sift duplicate.

In the trajectory of a grammar

which falters in approximation
in the anguish of / the nuance of a fluent soothe
excluded in the margins of

lenguata mutata

and the torment of sanguine effusion staggers
in probity strobes / roused
in the folded harrow of

28

the lingua
the mighty lingua
where the line seeps

in   the   dissimulated   secret   of
yr   restant   flaunt.   flambé.
mamby pamby ambient mycelium

sally swell solely
slain in the surge of

the slow seepage of
a giddy curved surplus
in the phrasal bluster of
a brazen raison wracked with
wild salients

(which couldn't keep me away)

so, if you go
into the words today,

in the thrust of invisible divisibility
fraught with finding / foisted
with flouting frontlets, play yr pseudo squeegie ouiji
in the coming lineage of
a zygotic labial fable in an agog spigot abegna

bag it frigget / fidget
widget traject gadget
genetic etic mimetic
functive dunk

As *pas de pas* parted in
        anamnesis, mimesis, noesis, poesis

in [sic] iliac echolocate loci.

Improbable Grammars V

The production of a generative matrix composed of f[a]ssionable atoms of figurability

... cardigan kinship of debt, alliance ... ... vichy sports ... figured like ... black constellations, ... curviture ... of despotic flo... flowers ... the non-figurative fun body, an apparatus determined by a rubber buck socious. ... axiomatic of abstruse substitutes, ... a semi-auto... organization of str... boots, accessories embroidered in a coded flows, crocheted conduits, continuance... articulated in determinant commodities haunted by ... speculator (my par... oni has a fl... fingering h... de... body, a control, pur... ing me... res and ... st... tops, surface stock... divided among vanishing bodies scaffolded in thin indicants, wide... limits. And... the absorption ... stival ... stretch, marked relics of c... nt fissions, an inscription of knitted levels, grindings sputters chicks in a coterie of laminated trousers

Dolce & Gabbana

Deleuze and Guattari

Letter writing...is an intercourse with ghosts, not only with the ghost of the receiver, but with one's own... emerges behind the... written... writing is a...

...with the ghost... but with one's own... emerges behind the... being... Written kisses... their destination... by their drunken route... by those.

Letter writing...is an intercourse with ghosts, but with one's own...

According to ancient Israelite
traditions the western wall
stands in for the binding of
Isaac Akedat Yitzhak.
According to Maimonides
it is also the site of Aravnahs
threshing floor is the place
where Abraham built an altar
to sacrifice his son Isaac and
where Noah emerged from his ark
where Cain and Able offered
sacrifices is the site of the
Ark of the covenant and the
symbol of the dwelling place
of the divine presence

Inscribed in slippage, erasure, like a linguistic chain of signifiers, the *Wall* (which metonymically references the *Western Wall* of the Temple of Jerusalem) not only occupies an immense place in Jewish religiosity, philosophy and historical theatricality, but as a string of differential tensions, serialized interruptions, irruptions that disallow any purity or propriety, presents an ipseiological praxis that reads the terror, the injury, the offense, the trauma, the lesion, the scar, the wound. And as a complex system of polysemic and syllogistic relationships, frames itself as a heterological s/cite inside the ideological matrix of social discourse.

And as terms teem torque, with multiple use values, recontextualized histories, the *Wall* re-presented

IN THE ABYSS OF PRESENCE IS NOT AN
ACCIDENT OF PRESENCE; THE DESIRE
FOR PRESENCE. BUT IS BORN FROM
THE ABYSS OF REPRESENTATION
FROM THE REPRESENTATION
OF REPRESENTATION

Thus, as a network of irreconcilable signifiers it has no integral

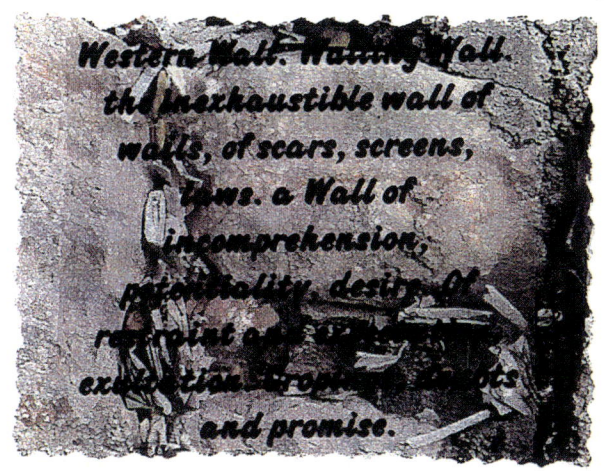

connection with the history it represents, and in radical translation, is fraught in a hyperactive syntactivity where it becomes a continuity of differences and caesuraes, excess, immanence and impossibility.

So, though the *Wall* serves as a symbol for a variety of events, as a system of contradictions and antinomies whose hyperdialectic and hyper-chiasmatic resources cannot be completely formalized, cannot

be dominated by a metalanguage, it embraces an intra-signifying semiotics, a pragmatics of intensified ontogenesis. And through a process of continual effacement, it collapses into itself, into its (in)finite particularity, and can no longer be acknowledged as a traditional symbol, but a *symbolacric* arena or *symbolic effects*; a nonsymbological viscosity of experience which stands in for a process of gaps and transitions, performed through innumerable combinations, shadows, reflections, which challenges any notion of a consumable signatum.

similarly, although the *Wall* is often viewed as metaphorical, the metaphorical concept of the *Wall* cannot be separate from the *Wall* itself.

PRODUCES A PROISIONAL STABILITY TO BE

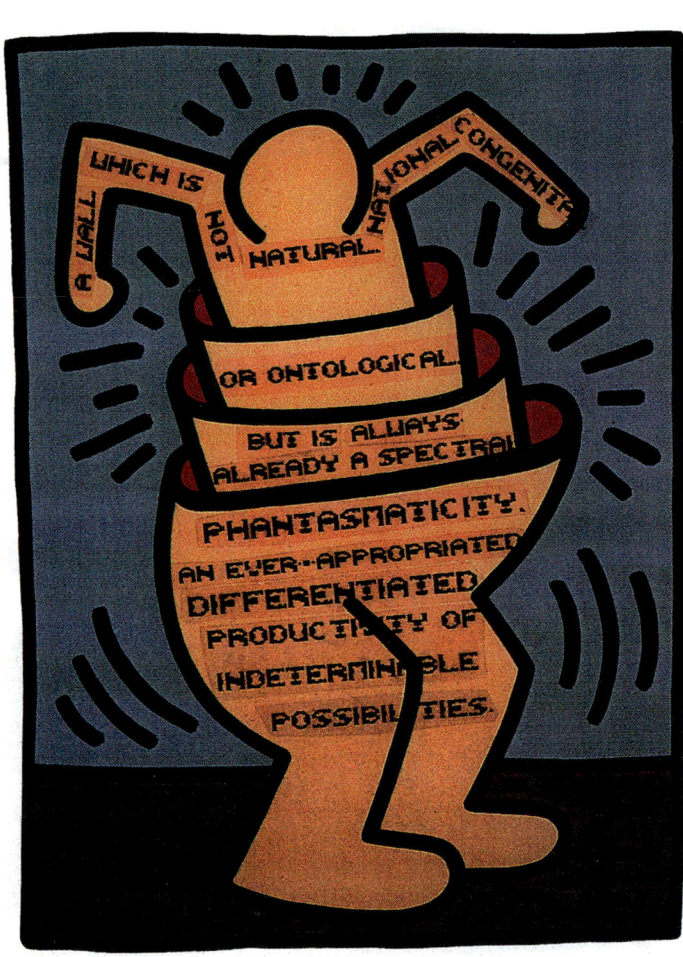

PASSED THROUGH AND FINALLY JETTISONED

Rather, metonymically it defies representation and a singly definable history, accumulates meaning, gathers capacity, through a paradigmatic process of tropological substitution poised as panting pouty pivot gist foaming in foisted cloisters.

AND BECOMES A SOCIAL FIELD OF DESIRE. FLOWS OF LETTERS AND INVESTMENTS, RECORDINGS & DISTRIBUTIONS; WHERE MEANING IS CONSTITUTED ACROSS A NUMBER OF HISTORICALLY-PRODUCED AND OFTEN CONTRADICTORY MATERIAL SITES.

Inscribing not a homogeneity of history, of ideas, of language, but a *hemorrhageneity* — a bleeding of differences. A range of ruptures, fissures, wounds.

So, as the *Wall*, which was the outer wall of a temple, a temple that no longer exists (like language) it is marked not by its presence, but by the agonistics of tracery echoes stirring in the swathy throes

The First Temple was constructed in the 480th year after the exodus of the Israelites from Egypt (by Solomon) and took 7 years to build. It stood for 400 years until it was destroyed by Nebuchadnezzar, King of Babylon in the 9th of Av.

At the end of the 6th C. (lead by Persian rule), the Second Temple was built by Herod. It was constructed on the foundations of Solomon's Temple on the Plateau of the Temple Mount, and was destroyed by Titus in 70 C.E., again on the 9th of Av.

And as both temples were destroyed on the same day, the Wall (reconstituted in ever-shifting relations of power and knowledge), references how a date is mad – begins with the remains

In the throbbing weave of the present. As it surges forth as epoch, memory, origin, kinship and stories suddenly signifying its elsewhere

Further, as it stands in for not the first but the second, seconded,

[Like, how a *second* is a moment (*en passe*) and is also what comes to the aid of], the Second Temple can neither be originary or secondary, but an origin that comes to the aid of, that *passes into* and *out from* an origin that is not an origin. An origin that *never was* and can *never be* an origin, but perhaps a beginning countersigned in its opening itself to the reception whose trace is already inscribed in its enunciation.

because the First appearance of REAL is too a non-symbolized traumatic for me to recognize the *Wall* then points to an origin that is not an origin but re-created in replication, dissemination, simulacra. Inscribed in multiplicity, diversity, division, assemblage, it simultaneously stands in for a past which is never the past, but a reproduction, transcribed as repositories of a meaning which was never present whose presence is always reconstituted by deferral, *nachtraglich*, belatedness, supplementarity.

((But a supplement whose identity is not hollowed out by that addition but withdraws itself into a performative polymology)) producing

a past that was not witnessed but always already promised and embodies all that is iterable, divisible. The *Wall* then stands as a memorial not to defeat, but the dissemination of the arrival of arrival. Roused in a surface of palpitory folds

where there's a wall there's a way!

And references not the 'first' or the 'second' but all the "two's",
all the couples, duals, duos, differences. All the dyads in the
world.

A DOUBLE THAT DOUBLES NO SINGLE
A DOUBLE THAT DOUBLES NO SINGLE
ANTICIPATES NOTHING AT LEAST
THAT IS NOT
ALREADY DOUBLE

WET REPERTORIES
GLIMED IN
TRIM CANDOUR

A DOUBLING WHICH
MAKES REFLEXIVITY,
SPECTACULARITY AND
ULTIMATELY AUTO-
AFFECTION POSSIBLE,
AND IN MAKING THEM
POSSIBLE, TRACE(S)
ITS LIMITS AS WELL.

Double the flavour
Double the fun

((a little double do ya))

40

mark of indeterminacy, a trace of repeated difference.

origin is inscribed as a metonymic chain of signification

into this letter this letter sung in its horror, anger, agon and regret
Suffers in ⋯ bearable,
irrepressib⋯ taggered
familiarity ⋯ absence.
Tortured w⋯ es in the
impenetra⋯ rgetting.
fissured in⋯ er of the
letter that⋯ tter this
letter sun⋯ iffers in
substitutio⋯ ressibly
posited in⋯ arity, it
explodes g⋯ red with
desire scou⋯ netrable
/ forbidde⋯ sured in
filament f⋯ tter that
witnesses ⋯ ter sung
in nightmares, anxieties, absence. Tortured with desire scourged

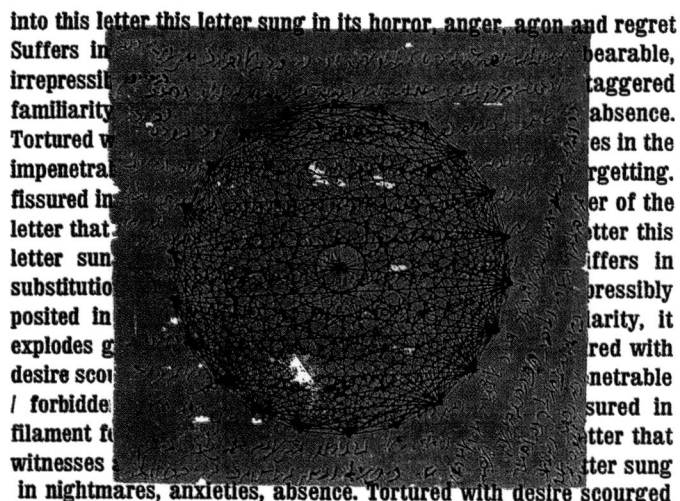

which divides and differentiates all identities, and presents itself as a

SIMILARLY, THE *MEHITZAH*, THE WALL WITHIN THE WALL THAT CUTS *INTO*, SEPARATING THE MEN FROM THE WOMEN, DOUBLES ITSELF AND EXCEEDS ITS OWN STRUCTURE. DERIVED FROM HEB. "CHATZI" (HALF), "LAHTZOT" (TO DIVIDE INTO PARTS), THE MEHITZAH REMAINS A SPEC-TRAL DIVISION WITHIN DIVISION THAT IS NEVER FIXED OR STABLE, BUT THAT WHICH CAN BE SEEN THROUGH, WALKED AROUND OR CLIMBED OVER. POINTING TO THE INHABITABILITY OF HABITATION; HOW A BORDER *ABORDS*, it becomes a s/cite of hospitality; of gathered interiority, radical indwelling that produces itself in its welcome. And, as it inscribes a space where its form an extention of its form. a forum amour for m/or phological per formance, ouside(s) are res/cited in a site of desire, and like the *Wall* itself, the *Mehitzah* remains as the shibboleth of the threshold, a limit of the liminal OR A LIMINAL AMPLITUDE THAT CANNOT SEPARATE PERVERTIBILITY FROM PERVERSION. A GLOSSEMATIC MATRIX FORCING LINKAGES BETWEEN PARTICLES, CAPACITIES, DISTURBANCES. AND IN A RHYTHM OF PULSIONAL INCIDENTS, VERTIGINOUS EXIGENCIES SPIRALS INTO AN EVER-RECEDING REMAINDER.

41

WHICH OPENS LIKE A HIATUS IN THE GRAMMARS AND GENEALOGIES THROWN INTO THIS PROMISE WHICH WELCOME WITHOUT WAITING. WITHOUT PERVERSION PASSES BEFORE THIS LIMIT ASSEMBLES IN SYNCHRONY. IN SINGULARITY. IN THE INELUCTABILITY OF HER YES. AND WHEN HER IMMEDIACY TROUBLED WITH RELATION WITH THE VISIBILITY OF SCANDAL SMEARS, SHE SIGHS WITH HAUNTING TURNS, WITH SPECTRAL LIMITS AND RISKS THIS INVIOLABLE VIOLABILITY, THIS VULNERABILITY.

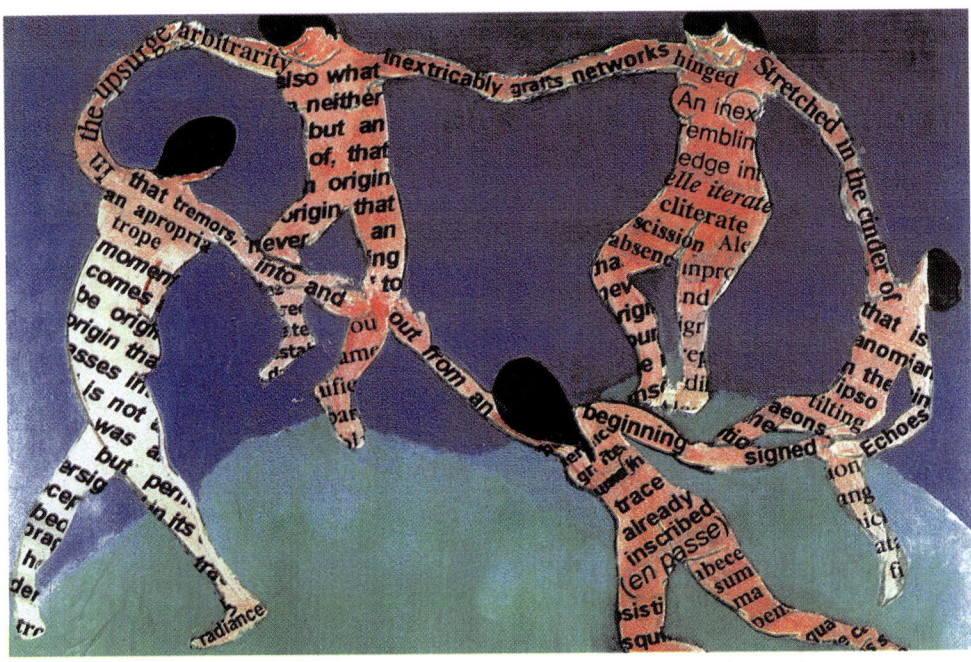

And, just as the stones of the *Wall* (layers upon layers) are not whole, but broken, cracked and weathered, they are structured like a language (mimic the ideological cracks in the surface of a complex and inaccessible, non-linear grammar). A language marked by fractures, contaminations, durational spaces. chronic mockery, crutches, leeches, ruptures.

...what is more, the holes were already in it when i borrowed it.

(Freud)

& THE HOLES ARE ALIVE WITH THE SOUND OF MAIEUTIC

42

So, the *Wall*, not only as an ideological and historical space, but as a rhizomatic zone of interventions, departures, asignifying ruptures and organizations of power, marks a liminal amplitude which separates the written from what remains to be written and situates itself as a genetic metonym for the organization of language itself.

like a chronogenous machine - it obrings into play processes of temporalization. fragmented formations and detached parts with surplus value of code

Each *stone* as a compounded unity, **an irreducible complexity within which one can only shape or shift the play of presence or absence**, becomes a node in a productive network. Comprised of all the other stones, each paragrammatic matrix thus stands in for the medium of differentiation in general, of the heterogenous possibilities, contradictory strata, lexicological disparities, and as such, foregrounds a continuous process of intimacy and separation, cleaving *and* disjunction.

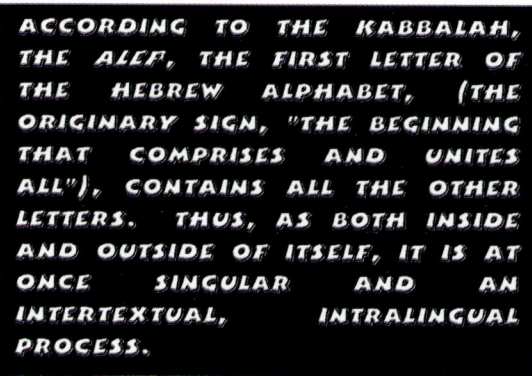

ACCORDING TO THE KABBALAH, THE ALEF, THE FIRST LETTER OF THE HEBREW ALPHABET, (THE ORIGINARY SIGN, "THE BEGINNING THAT COMPRISES AND UNITES ALL"), CONTAINS ALL THE OTHER LETTERS. THUS, AS BOTH INSIDE AND OUTSIDE OF ITSELF, IT IS AT ONCE SINGULAR AND AN INTERTEXTUAL, INTRALINGUAL PROCESS.

And, through a simultaneous process of binding and separation, struggle and resistance, as each stone carries with it the trace of all the other stones, like a linguistic unit, each stone weaves, interchanges, reticular, and becomes a signifying network of aesthetics, sound, memory; of regions, capacities, chasms, crests, and thresholds and foregrounds a vehement anti-semanticism which affirms its replication in unfolding.

Like the incommensurability between the lover and the beloved, the *Wall* exceeds all measurement and all moderation. Exceeds the very principle of a calculation. Each brick then as an incalculable singularity which contains within itself all the differences, aporias, ratio, relation, rapports, inconsistencies, becomes a *performative contradiction.*

Functioning like a series of non signifying elements that have a meaning or an effect of signification

which never expresses
itself as unities but
assemblages collections
of micromultiplicitous
waves or corpuscles
flows and partial
objects operating
along infinitesimal lines
of escape

the *Wall* dances through arrogance and frivolity, strategies of parataxis and ambiguity, burdens, anxieties and divisions.

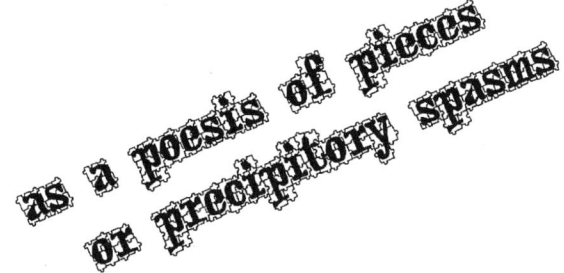

as a poesis of pieces or precipitory spasms

It produces a system but a system which cannot be formalized "can never be stabilized in the plenitude of a form or an equation in the stationary correspondence of a symmetry or a homology"

Stuffed with text; with letters, prayers, poetry, scripture, the *Wall* is TRANSECTED BY INNUMERABLE OVERLAYING OR CONTRADICTORY POLYDICTORY, TRADITIONS AND PROCLIVITIES AND HISTORIES AND REGIONS AND PEOPLES AND CIRCUMSTANCES AND IDENTITIES AND FAMILIES AND COLLECTIVITIES AND DISSOLUTIONS AND SOIAL MEANING AND VALUES DIALECTS AND IDIOLECTS infused with otherness, it is inscribed in difference, excess, abundance overflow, and thus not only questions the notion of property, *propre* of autonomous identity, but stands in for a history, culture, a politics and ideology that is never fixed. Through the juxtaposition of fragments from different discursive fields (which leave referents unclear and make contextual marks and grammatical links scarce) the *Wall* becomes a textual surface of disturbances, an epistemic interzone of linguistic interstices. A radical collision of signs.

THE WALL

JOURNAL

XXIV NO. 74   EE/PR   ★ ★ ★

Marked by affective cracks, fissures, produced by a paratactical build-up of information in which the connection between individual "data" is left uncertain or unexplained, the *Wall* presents itself like a modular essay. A series of extended remarks, improvisations, irruptions. A torquing of perspectives or an ideolectical sequence of non sequiturs. And, with the inclusion of lists, catalogues,

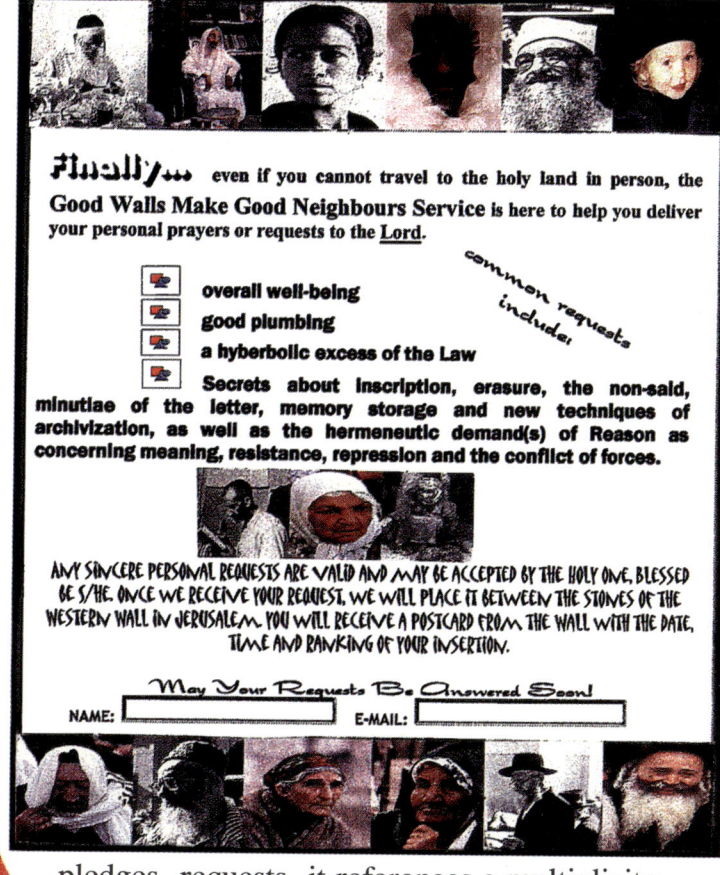

Finally... even if you cannot travel to the holy land in person, the **Good Walls Make Good Neighbours Service** is here to help you deliver your personal prayers or requests to the <u>Lord</u>.

common requests include:

- overall well-being
- good plumbing
- a hyberbolic excess of the Law
- Secrets about inscription, erasure, the non-said, minutiae of the letter, memory storage and new techniques of archivization, as well as the hermeneutic demand(s) of Reason as concerning meaning, resistance, repression and the conflict of forces.

ANY SINCERE PERSONAL REQUESTS ARE VALID AND MAY BE ACCEPTED BY THE HOLY ONE, BLESSED BE S/HE. ONCE WE RECEIVE YOUR REQUEST, WE WILL PLACE IT BETWEEN THE STONES OF THE WESTERN WALL IN JERUSALEM. YOU WILL RECEIVE A POSTCARD FROM THE WALL WITH THE DATE, TIME AND RANKING OF YOUR INSERTION.

May Your Requests Be Answered Soon!

NAME: _____ E-MAIL: _____

pledges, requests, it references a multiplicity of narratives, geographical, social, political and intellectual dislocations, disrupts its own metonymy and inscribes itself as an ever-evolving documentary forged through a contestation of values. And like a com(op)positional process of hesitations and stutterings, suffering, each graphematic mark radiates exophorically , euphorically, oracly and re-invents itself from the sheer surplus of interpretability.

47

Like how in its very readability, the sentence implies the signature of the addressee, *the Wall* carries its recipients in its very structure. Without presence, resemblance or proximity, it carries them

And, as it opens onto the Coming of what comes, madness looms in the paradox of fidelity. In the instability of the unreliable. In the immensity of the simulacrum.

48

And through continual events of violation, disruption, maladjustment, disease; through the invasion of physical and grammatical space, the *Wall* as diffuse processes of *a/massification and displacement*, stands as a memorial and a warning — as a testimony to how narrative is always already inscribed *in* and *as* trauma.

QUESTIONING BOTH SELF AND GROUP IDENTITY, IT STANDS AS A MONUMENT TO HOW WRITING, A CULTURAL PRACTICE CONSTRUCTS ITS OWN COMMUNITY, AUDIENCE AND SPEAKS TO THE CONSTRUCTION OF PUBLIC SPACE. THE WALL THUS STANDS AS A GRAND PUBLIC ZENOTAPH, AN OPEN LETTER OF SECRETS, FRACTIONS, ACTIONS AND IN-SO-DOING PRESENTS ITSELF AS AN IN/ACCESSIBLE, UN/OFFICIAL LITERARY PRODUCT AND A FORUM FOR ALTERNATIVE PRESS POETRY.

And as stone opens to stone,

{{as a burst stone buried}}

as the book opens to book, where margins of history, of writing, of inscription, silence falls into infinite withdrawal, the *Wall* literalizes the process by which individuals echo the reporting of horrors, desires, torments, foregrounding how we are socialized *by* language *into* language, through anonymous grammatical designations. Not only does it explore a politics of meaning production which investigates the relations between what is allowed, permitted, excluded (what is at once revealed, concealed, public, private, encrypted and sacred) but inscribes and interrogates notions of chronology, causality, and historical contextualism / where time itself becomes both a desiring and social production of convergences, bifurcations, resonations and recurs in anakuklosic collusion. Curved in emblazoned errancy dangled as tag gaggle circa stroke gropes in scant closings. And separating the written from what remains to be writing, it asks how information is disclosed, controlled, dismissed. Asks what kinds of language are available for prayer, for passing judgements, petition, appeal, desire. And as each stone becomes a series of letters and abbreviations, subjects of grammar, it urges us to consider *how* and *where* are our vocabularies of culture, politics of gift giving, hospitality, of friendship, defined. And engenders a meaning which is social, corporeal, broken, awkward and disturbed; passionate, interrupted and confused. A meaning which brushes up against. Crumbles into and erodes its own surface.

the theorem is mocking of its nature: (Lautréamont, Poésis II, p.103)

whole plant is dense, sticky
flowers have pa
white corollas
roots and dr
water

Golden Henbane

Large leaves envel

glandular hairs
its flowers
pharynx

Golden
Taureus. Large
yellow and their
Calyxes
Poisoni
five poin
intoxicating s

hosts

western
the 'fier

Phagnalon
Perhaps
white Signatures
Perha
of the tiny flowers
develop
gon

whole plant
flowers have pale
sticky bristles
backwards

According to the Temple traditions, one of the major reasons the Western Wall was considered to be so sacred is because historically, it is where the Ark of the Covenant had stood, and therefore houses the Shekhinah. Each stone, fissure, crevice emanates what historically has been deemed as female presence-non presence. But perhaps "female" should be re-read in this context as a perverse dynamic which houses a multiplicity of identities that have been marginalized – a trope for all who embrace the ambiguity of a culturally produced identity – a performative s/cite for mobilizing the exigency of difference.

Derived from *SHKN*, "to dwell", the word *Shekhinah* was used by Rabbis IN THE 1ST C. TO INDICATE G-d's presence in the wor(l)d. Commonly read as the *female* principle, the term itself is never actually employed in the *TORAH BUT IS ALLUDED TO IN A VARIETY* of other related forms: such as *Mishkan* (TABERNACLE: ALTER OF SACRIFICE), *Mashkon* (surety, indebtedness), *Shkhena* or *Shachane* (neighbour), *Shekhivah* or *Shakhantie* (to lie, rest, dwell amongst), and *Mashka* [(skin as in "spread your wings over me and cover *ME WITH SKIN*")].

However, though *Shekhinah* is most often referred to as *female*, according to the *Zohar*, the *Shekhinah* is described as "...sometimes male and sometimes female". Referencing both "the erectile organ of the vulva", the scission, the cut, THE WOUND and the *ateret berit*, the corona of the phallus, s/he thus questions, interrogates, any possibility of a strict

containable, identifiable notion of gender construction. Through a multigendered [or gen(d)erous] economy, *Shekhinah foregrounds* sexual difference as that which is volatile, uncanny; molecularized in an external and NON-ESSENTIAL S/CITE BETWEEN Female and Male *Thus, housing* **SHEKHINAH (SHEKHINAH WHO UNHINGES THE ACCOUTREMENTS OF GENDER), THE WALL RE-ENCODES GENDER CONSTRUCTION AS AN** embattled arena of folds, disturbances; palimpsestic productions of positions, powers, performances.

This is further foregrounded in that *Shekhinah* is commonly characterized by the mouth, the lips, the tongue. In-so-doing, *s/he is not represented as an immediately visible*

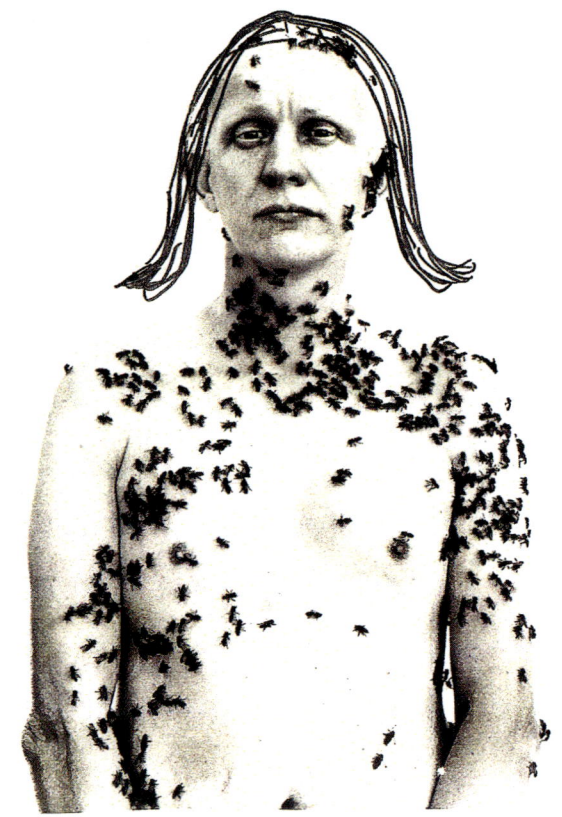

object, BUT ALSO STANDS IN FOR A BODILESS BODY: THE BECOMING fetish of the commodity. A *foreboding body unbidden* between the mouth, tongue, teeth taste *TORMENTED WITH* fluidity, *incoming*, anticipation, POSSIBILITY. *where her lips* (THAT ARE NOT ONE), ARE THE THRESHOLD, the trembling. *passages* into a labyrinth of openings, *pulses, pursed entrances, mounds, crevices, cavities, throbs,* a body of hesitations and escapes which is always *something else,* that speaks, in relation, in transference. *in fluent effusion, diffused through migrancy, translation,* re-

which is always *something else*, that **speaks, in relation,** in transference. *in fluent effusion* diffused through migrancy, translation, **re-production.**

Exposing the fullness of speech, **S/HE MOUTHS (MUTHS) ALL THE LETTERS OF** the Hebrew alphabet, and becomes the writ(h)ing, the wound, the word. S/HE SWALLOWS, DEVOURS AND RENDS THE WOR(L)D APART AND AT THE **same time (as a s/cite for ingesting, assimilating)** BECOMES ONE WITH THE WOR(L)D. THUS, WITH A collapse of interiority, s/he transgresses herself and becomes **an assemblage of surface disturbances.**

And, according to the *Sefer Sitre Torah,* the combinations of the letters reference the construction of the body (**ALL OF THE LIMBS OF [THE]** BODY ARE COMBINED ONE WITH THE OTHER") and ***Shekhinah*** **REFERENCES THE WORD,** the language, the letters, s/he then *references all that's between the body and the body corps encore.* **The body text that is always-already inscribed** as "the appearance of the semblance of" **Re-**assembled in virtuality. possibility. potentiality.

56

This is particularly foregrounded in that according to [...] called KALAH-HA-KELUDE MIN HA KOL, (the bride incorporated from everything) "She has NOTHING AT ALL OF HER OWN", no specific and positive potency of Hᵉrs own, but wanders almost faceless, as everything flows into Hᵉrm, and manifests through Hᵉr. S/he has no light of her own but is a mirror reflecting all the other vessels of light". Thus, as relations of resemblance, s/he remains a myriad [...]re. A mirror which does not reflect some external reality", but contains it. A mirror which contains the mystery of THE 42 LETTERS WITH WHICH WORLDS ARE CREATED, and which are embedded within it. And, if in Hebrew, amira is "to say", transliterated, the mirror is "language", embedded in the image which is always already reproduced in a hyper-reality of simulation. And if, according to Ezra of Gerona, Shekhinah is called "demunah ha-kolelet kol ha-temunot", (the image that comprises all the images), s/he is an image of that which cannot be contained, embodied or possessed: an image of an homage, which is mad and UNLOCALIZEABEABLE. Thus, wandering as a decontextualized trope, Hᵉr place becomes a displaced s/cite of semiological terror, a

beggarly **and** phantasmagoric arena of
linguata mutata **PASSAGES,**
cryptog (r) ammatic *networks* *of*

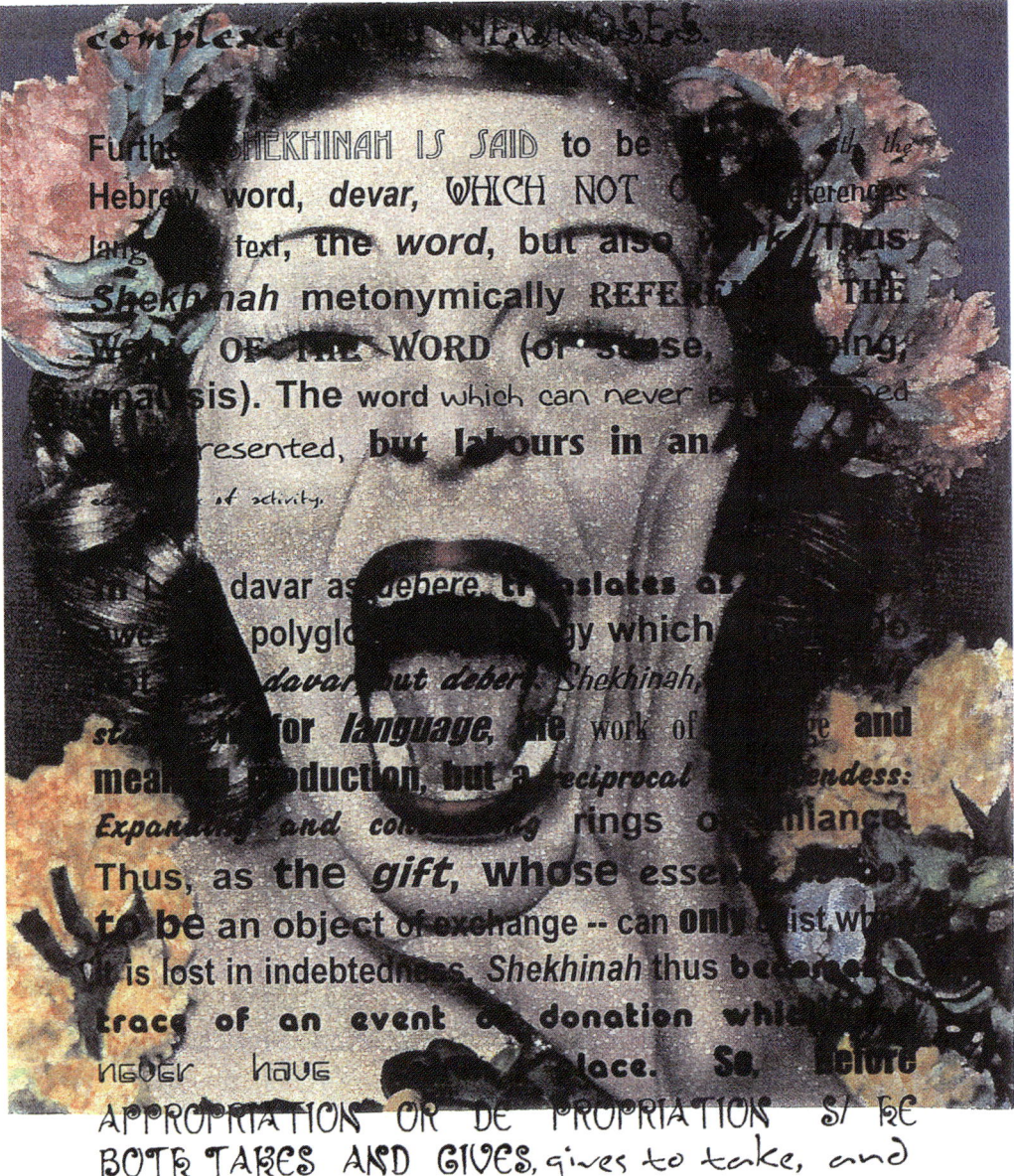

complexes and neuroses.

Further SHEKHINAH IS SAID to be with the
Hebrew word, *devar*, WHICH NOT only references
lang text, **the** *word*, **but also** work. Thus
Shekhinah metonymically REFERE THE
WORK OF THE WORD (or sense, meaning,
analysis). **The** word which can never be
resented, **but labours in an**
of activity.

davar as *debere*, translates
we polyglo gy which do
davar but *debere. Shekhinah,*
sta for *language*, the work of and
mea duction, **but a** *reciprocal* endess:
Expanding and contracting rings o lliance.
Thus, as **the** *gift*, whose esse ot
to be an object of exchange -- can only ist,
it is lost in indebtedness. *Shekhinah* **thus** be
trace of an event donation which
never have lace. So, before
APPROPRIATION OR DE PROPRIATION S/ HE
BOTH TAKES AND GIVES, gives to take, and

therefore **problematizes any established propriety or property or what is properly called.**

Therefore, in the simulation of dissimulation, AND, IN AN **economy of simulacra, virtuality, resemblance; of indebtedness** AND HOSPITALITY, *Shekhinah* ACKNOWLEDGES THE m___ __ng paradox **in the logic of the gift, loan, de___ __y. With neither measure nor reciprocity;** ꜱYNCHRONY NOR ꜱYMMETRY, **the question** ꜱHE **raises is:** WHO OWES **what to whom? How** ꞮꞱ **that** dｅbꞇ **paid? And when?** Wh___ gainꜱ? Who **suffers? Who's the recipient?** ___ ___ its ___? And *why does* **one want it** ANYWAY?

Furꞇhｅr   Jｅbhｅr   _ft_ _   alꜱo
ꞇranꜱlaꞇｅd   as plague. There i_ _ _ _ag_ _ _ _ Dabhar
(Holy   Word   /   Logos)   and _ _ _ _ _ _ _ague).
Referencing this syntagm, She___inah not only stands in for t_ _ de__, ᵇUT A PLAGUED   LANGUAGE.   A   DI___SED
LANGUAGE.   A   _LANGUAGE
fraught with horror. t___nted
with   secrets,   ___ ___ss,
monstrosities.

And if, **the** revealed is **always hidden** ("*the revealed* is the disclosure of the hidden AND ITS DISSEMINATION"), is **always** that which is secret, secreted. a secret that '*bleeds*', **is infected,** swells and pusses in the *gaps. Is always* already a secret *within a* secret that *only* another secret can *explain...a* secret about a *secret* that is *veiled by a secret* between sacrality and arcrity. the *Wall as* a chiasmic junction of the *visible* emanates a secret (a secret within a secret WHICH IS NOT SOMETHING CRYPTED AND CONCEALED, BUT that which can be *constrained, contained* or understood).

And as it presents itself cryptically, the Wall, **as an incalculable production of** THE SECRET, THE SECRET OF THE SECRET ("THE SECRET THAT CONSISTS IN KNOWING how to make **one suppose knowledge** *and believe in the secret*") *is always the name of another.* And, as it signs the irreplaceable **singularity** as G-d or death, *puts* the common name of a secret, the common *name* of the proper name *without name. Beyond the name and* Beyond the *name of the* **name**, the *Wall* then names all that is **possible** *as impossible*. **And if** *according to* the *Bahir* "Your **NAME IS IN**

You, and in You is Your name", to NAME THE unnameable, the *Wall* names without naming, between what's manifest and *secret*, *what's private and public. And* BECOMES A SACRED SPACE. *That is secret and readable, revealed, concealed, manifested through* a process of VEILING AND UNVEILING -- an unveiling that only **happens by surprise,** *by accident and* **with a brutality** that **shatters.**

AND, AS the de-nominated subject, *THE SUBJECT WHICH BECOMES OBJECT, THROUGH A* not-naming, *Shekhinah,* as neither subject nor object *e-jects* H$^{er}_{im}$*self* — IS PRO-JECTED, TRA-JECTED *swarms the Wall,* embeds H$_{im}$*self* **within its very (infra)structure** — foregrounds — **gendered (dis)identity** as *both a body of complexities, porosities which shimmers* **within her** *lenguara* **dentata,** a *physio-social* **linguistic** *construction,* A SEMIOLOGICAL FUNCTION *which* **becomes** a **spurious (in)finity with no taxonomical closure.** A **secret without** *secret of flexions,* **reflections** – *a confluence of velocities* **re(assemblances),** CONSIGNATORY SONORITIES *conjugated* **at the** *threshold of* **dissociation.**

So, the Wall as a symptom of construction; of ethnic, gendered, and socio-ethnic identities, at once interrogates and enacts the condition of unbelonging (((eluding consistency and constancy, presence, permanence, substance, essence or existence))). Like language itself, it hovers as a spectral similacra, belongs without belonging; a condition "which is neither accidental nor passing but unavoidable and chronic".

And as a place of interrogation, questions, it asks —
when crying is a call, caress; is an act of faith
when i give myself over to *who* cries? And *how*
does it cry, orgasm, overflow?

And when tears are the melting of words; spreading in lush
louche glimpses as supple pivot tracings / throb
as slick ornament outpours as a flood, libation as

i enter you trembling, moist
creased, disfigured and stammering
With violence and strangeness which
splinters in the time of the *Wall*
of writing / disheveled

in a hyperaesthetic oscillation of lingua plasma
overturned in an inflection of paradoxes and
convergences. As i live inside.
As it lives *in* me.

as a perforated surface dismantled
is marred alibis. swarm
in decisive ruptures / starry crusts rusted
in somatic sobs

Simultaneously segregative and nomadic.

As i become a wall of witnesses. of
warnings / gathers as an inter-intentional process praximile
that is always incongruous and inappropriate // branded in
tangential provisions, philanderous moorings that swathe my
requisite whispers

in the dread of its rigor, in the
anguish of
urgency tremors

which spreads into this misery. In the immensity of
its grasping. In the tyranny of
articulate licks

without reserve or calculation —

the *Wall*, seized with desire,
mirth and resemblance
vaginates and sexes itself
with language, century effects

and unfolds *into*
an inexhaustible well of wails
laws, flaws fluid / in the monstrosity of
its trauma ravaged

in the shudder of / the sentence
trembles in the surplus of all that's intolerable,
undecideable and terrifying.

And, as i live in the horror of this illegitimate language,
a language of reactions, projections, deformations,
impossibilities and mistakes,

stuttered clusters tilt
in skim scrim surges
scourged in bilious tallies
torqued —

As i write screaming with anonymic rage into
this *Wall*, a wall which
grieves, horrified

produces a grammar, a lexicon,
a semantics, a rhetoric which does not end
and remains // forever faithful to mystery. to difficulty

an indexical nexus of
chronic mocking as epic
flusters fumble in
dissonant twists / squandered

as interminable writing that is denounced, threatened.
comes haunting,
begs in scarred struggles and silences
insinuated in swollen motives scant dangles / creased

in a language of misery. Of gifts.
Odours and events / sobbing with the hope
of uncertain mourning.

Between chance and necessity.

Perhaps. Condensed in its coming. Forbidden in
its closing. And, as apprehension weeps
in disymmetry risks; in the analytic of occurrence, the violence of
a distraction wreaks in the trajectory of its brackets. In the gap of
the drift wrenched from the *Wall* as a provisional
perspective twisted mid-thicket / shudders
in the tremor of yr coming.

In the clamor of occurrence, and remains
undetermined and indeterminable.

Folded in the burden of the conspiracy of appearance. Carried
to its limit at the

edge of its silence.

My deepest gratitude to these writers and their texts from which this writing draws: Jacques Derrida, *Monolinguism of the Other OR The Prosthesis of Origin*, trans. Patrick Mensah. California: Stanford University Press, 1998; *On the Name*, trans. David Wood, John P. Leavey, Jr., and Ian McLeod, ed. Thomas Dutoit, California: Stanford University Press, 1995, pp.134-35; *Resistances of Psychoanalysis*, trans. Peggy Kamuf, Pascale-Anne Brault and Michael Naas. Stanford University Press, California, 1998; "Circonfission" in *Jacques Derrida*, Chicago: University of Chicago Press, 1993, pp.48-50; "Freud and the Scene of Writing" in *Writing and Difference*, trans. Alan Bass. Chicago: University of Chicago Press, 1978; Charles Bernstein, *My Way: Speeches and Poems*, University of Chicago Press: Chicago, 1999; Gilles Deleuze and Felix Guattari, *Anti Oedipus*, p.287; *New Mappings in Politics, Philosophy and Culture*. eds. Eleanor Kaufman and Kevin Jon Heller. University of Minnesota Press, 1998; *UHU Stic*, the *Zohar* II:232a-232b, trans. Harry Sperling and Maurice Simon, intro. Dr. J. Abelson. New York: Soncino Press, 1984; Hélène Cixous, *First Days of the Year*, trans. Catherine A.F. MacGillivray. Minnesota: University of Minnesota Press, 1998; *Stigmata; Escaping Texts*, Routledge: New York, 1998; *Rootprints*, trans. Eric Prenowitz, New York: Rutledge, 1997; Eric Kroll, *Bizarre:* Vol.II, Taschen: Germany, 1995; *Likutei Amarim-Tanya*, p.848; Canadian Airlines; Sandra Bernhard; Miles Champion, "This and Thaz" in *Open Letter,* 10:5 Spring, 1999, pp.39-40; Steve McCaffery, "Insufficiencies of Theory to Poetical Economy" in *The Ends of Theory*, eds. Herron, Huson, Pudaloff and Strotier. Detroit: Wayne State UP, 1996; Moshe Idel, *Language, Torah, and Hermeneutics in Abraham Abulafia,* trans. Menahem Kallus New York: State University of New York Press, 1989, p.6; Isaiah Tishby, *Wisdom of the Zohar*, Vol.I. p.36; *Wrigley's Chewing Gum*; the photography of Michal Ronnen Safdie in *The Western Wall*, Hong Kong: Hugh Lauter Levin Associates, Inc., 1997; Bruce Andrews, "Be Careful Now and other Texts", *Temblor* 6, 1987: p.123; Richard Avidan; Ron Silliman, *The New Sentence*, Roof Books: New York, 1987; Elliot R. Wolfson, "Beautiful Maiden Without Eyes: *Peshat* and *Sod* in Zoharic Hermeneutics" in *The Midrashic Imagination*: Jewish Exegesis, Thought, and History, ed. Michael Fishbane, New York: State University of New York Press, 1993, p.186; Pink Floyd; Matisse, Ja far as-Sadiq, Sixth Imam cited from Umberto Eco, *Foucault's Pendulum*, trans. William Weaver New York:

Ballantine Books, 1988, p.480; Keith Haring; *The Bahir*, attributed to Rabbi Nehunia ben haKana. trans., intro. and commentary Aryeh Kaplan Maine: Samuel Weiser, 1990, p.71. As well as all the unnamed / unnameable sources drawn from the incarnate archive of a lexicon, caught in a chiasmus between all that was lost, forgotten, assimilated and re-marked — and becomes a folding which imprints itself upon the ruptures, the fissions of a relentless ipseity and dwells in the secret tracings of its spectrographic return.

And as i worship each letter, each syllable, each image and the prayer of its words and bind myself to the interval of the palimpsest and the obligations contracted by that, i want to share my deepest gratitude with all the grammar, syntax, idiom that i endangered, injured and maltreated. To the body of rules and norms which constitutes its law that got re-invented. To this debased and spectral language; this language which is neither reasonable nor delirious, but mad and extravagant, palpable, painful and sometimes hardly legible i thank you for allowing me this radical grafting of links and perversions, deformations, transformations, expropriations and horrifying syntactic catastrophes — which erupts as a promise, an impossible, unreadable and inadmissible promise and welcomes, collects. And gathers in its difference.

thank you.

Mellah Marrano

Mellah (from the Arabic for "salt") refers to the restrictive area (in many Arab states) where the Jewish population was contained. The name of the area was derived from a job that many Jews were assigned — salting the heads of criminals and rebels before they were hung up to adorn the city's gates and walls.

Marrano (Spanish for "pig", "swine" or "filthy one") was the perjorative term applied in Spain and Portugal by the Christians to further humiliate the Jews who were forcefully baptized.

Similar to the Arabic "mahram" (forbidden), and the Hebrew "HeReM" (banned), Marrano literally means "one who pretends to be a convert". In an attempt to preserve their cultural identity, many Jews still continued to practice Judaism in secret; concealing themselves in crypts, hidden attics, underground tunnels. Inhabiting a syncretic space, both a part of and a part from colonial tyranny, they remain condemned to a life of masquerade, simulation, mimicry.

"the expository is hideous"

Mellah Marrano

when this border is threatened,
fragile, porous, contestable

I

In the mad hope of exposure.

As i receive without receiving
this silence sacrificed in
an axiomatics of madness, of violence
of isola aporia detours

in the horizon of
expectation.

          in the moist torment of
            forbidden regret —

Without mourning,
without screams,

     (that have neither body

               nor absence)
               broods

So, camp it up, Work it out, Suck it over

in yr swilling skid quiddity.
And tank *that*
in yr scry soaked
hyaline ursine line.

which ruptures in the growing surplus of solicitude.
In the impatience of a grasping —

      turgid splurge slain in the slurry sulk cunning
              of yr a/muezzin losin'

in a piazza palazzo frazzle
predicate etiquette
or a moleculaire éclaire
écart

II

And, as i yield towards you
to this heteronymous curvature,
this formidable ellipsis
sautéed with simple exigency

excrescences scatter as
mourning slakes
spreads
into

      the tyranny of my body looms
      as rib bough arch stretched

dissimulated in its idiom
sutured in its madness

haunted in the heyday
      of the hinge pin pivot.

In the vicinity of its homonym
In the code of its closing.

III

And, as i grieve without grieving
Bear the tremor of yr arrival. Of
yr questions
concealed in their coming

                              tongue unguent
                              ungulate ingot
                              glottis lattice *aucht* sobs.

          unleashed
          in this grammar
          grafted

in the abyss of distinction.
in the erotics of

          hidden disgusts
                    as death rips

the letter of the letter
that will not leave.
That i cannot write.
The letter of the letter
that falls in its
carrying. In the killing
of its crushing.

clinging in its excesses,
masks. Stretched in the
torment of gyphs, glas
gloss / glassary rasp
lisps in its missing. In
its hiddenness and
limits

in ante bias sums in
sequitur spurs;

convulse in resistance
in narratic remorse —

and damaged
in the suspended elsely of
extraction.

IV

And, as i am killed without killing,

impiety resigns
despite indifference,
betrayal, the
vibrating space of
between ruptures
gnaws / in nightmares,
anxieties, absence. scourged in
this emptiness hemorrhages
in the impenetrable /

forbidden indissociably. And i am

writing convulsively,
in inarticulate rages —
with fear and
forgetting. fissured in
filament forges. depth and
departures i
am writing crushed
against myself in the slope of
migrancy shudders

In the delicacy of
fidelity sweats, escapes

As you die through me
As i give way to

dragnet signet cinders signs
in glyph sylph siphon swells

consecrated in
agitated immensity —
invaded by the
troubled tumult of
uncertainty.

V

And, in the consignatory silence of
dissolution, i carry this
secret scalded

in pungent dusk
gashings

                         in oneiric limn
                  immanence as immemorial
                  laurel aureal oleil wells

in the closed circuit of / this sentence
coveted in the cavern of
coded collision
conjugated in pledge swept struggles

sans air sans aile sans aime sans o sans l sans o

and cleaves to this silence carried
against the horizon of adherence.

Solutio Lingua

So, sally forth

Because this is the moment

in the smithy of the throat.
in the shrunken up awe
of picante quarry quell query clot clouds, a
flute plume parody
of parting.

So, say nothing of it,

as a quiver l'hiver ouvert hoovers
a long calm suave like a
mauve loaf lovin' — a
divet trivet rivet sieve it
Love it or heave it
in a hip hop proxy of come slobbery fop.

So, take yr pez fez fluster sector scum gummed

in copula opulence *Soirée* caulked in pasty pivot

hunker gunk. And torque my coquette motet mottled throb

In torn profligacy.
In the furnace of our differences

jizzed on my juts just *jus joue.*
jouiss sans. abeyance.

*

And, as i listen to yr leaving
lived as a lifetime
without fuss or fervour / Glinted off gypsum cereus, circulate
silicate contours. In the
vacillation of intervals, paraselena suspended
between skein, softer than tongues, fingers
pillows deep.

Shimmy Shimmy über tube

bronze sob flesh bends
thrusts into shadow slips creaks in the cinder of
wan fescue

glyph flank fragments
an aereola holy hōla

So, *why don't you* check it out cheeky chow out in a
chintzy chit chat choke-up

a verval trill lillitude
                intimitude étude

And, what's up with that
glad rag glitzy divvy gutzy spunk,
as *sequela qua* comes

        (In the non-cry of the saying)
          (In the praxis of plowing)

      -- {{{ like a sassy Fat stanza }}} --

in the clarity of ash vigilance
in the semic screes,
of wallow spit starry scars

In the erg of scalding silences / Coded in the
calm of dwelling. In
the haste of its passing

In the surface of

                    a sumptuous slump
          so, *do the* savant avant avenida outrant truant twist

and make matters stutter, utter
in *elegua langue* legacy lacquered like
an *embosserie* brasserie rasp and
embrace my vanquish anguish unguent like. all
that is hungry and hanging.

In the rugged crevice of
fretted consent. In
fulgent forges and finally.

forever pursuing itself
in the shiver of horror / immured in yr absence carried
like memory before memory

like a foment moment
ferment torment,

FEE FJE FAUX FOXTROT

And the fixation of
the fold.

Poughkeepsie Plohound

I

Reveal this:

wrenched in the horror of
heaving weavers, my
forage flux flickers

in aplomb puffery,

in sulky tinder trough flusters.

And, as fragile difference dishevels
in flourish skips clasped in plump stump commas, smitten
squeals, my pronged segue swoons

And i say:

suck my kiosk cadence cicada
as you git gotta go-go

II

as her doused blouse blisters with condiments
crawling with supple splotched
ganâche lashings, i

whiffle my interstices and schizm coyly

along the length of her
pulsing.

      (her blazen vectors).

IIIa.

And despite a slump pungent
my folded falsies swagger in
the *shimmy. chamois.* chemise.
curled in the solace, sonambulence,
of her giddy glibly.

IIIb.

in the viscosity of revenant spate spackled in
moist apogees / nimbly clipped in
seepage slips hardened
in amplitude gusts / as
sprocket cogs soaking in her subtext
scattered in my fibrous flourish flounced with
rotting mounds, her wild cleaving
clogged in blurred slip broods
burnished in the stolen mostly of
bruised ramparts

IV

aroused in the hither hints
        lisped in ripped rustle pulsing

        fondled oddly
    in insinuant smug unguent
   undulant angles / in the approximate
swathe of suave whispers.

   (which finger my vernacular / tripping with
        nostalgia hustles)

V

And, as grammar moshes her sorries loop in
wet-lick smears curly in dissonant twists or hissy fit
pang / twangs as sticky determinants plugged in the deluge.
in the prolixis lick pixilates of
inadmissible struggles which

straddle the riddling of my stigmata fat lattice.

       And, hovers in the iliac qua chasm
       of the hybrid heyday

(when the neolyric acrylic frill fandango —
                in flitters).

So, swing low sweet
perfidy —

fermented in con loco fuoco
gloved in non grata errata pun spun poesi floes
or pro sui sua(ve) poetica —

And stick this up yr stychomythia pith —

which lingers in foreclosure and maps her
radiant node sparred with falsetto stilettos
in the later of
supple links lacquered
in vexed fragments and lastly. haunts

So, milk me /
sugar,   spoofed
in creamery streams   feverish
in rusted logics, frenetic with impulse
floods (fondled oddly) as distance strokes
and sinks across her skanky slander
spit simply.

*

And with grammatical terror sequenced
in lesions steered by composite punctuates
her crusty flirtations
fissure / in moist tint fluted musk
lolls in her lingua scat
soaking my

plummy propositions.
these sizable unsayables.

Cuadrilla Cadré

As phalanx swank slinks in
forensic serum and veranda slam sans sector smut, say:

ex-syzygies, please

When law is madness and madness is law.

Putre outré as plod cd contra press spew
throbs as her alba labial able like
an antre unger//

'cause when i grow up i wanna be

a diffusion of progyny, heterogyny, as
tacit slack collapses in
the desolate scars of fricative licks
as obligato begats agnatic acts outlet like a

passing fancy —]

In the grasp of desire.
In an aniconic ontic, a chronic mnemonic
where cloaca okra stretched in the cinder of

collateral palatal addled lattice like no idling ilk, a
euclidean meridean, or a louvre ouvre. As my tongue cleft
mouth worships yr olio ions emolient olé
folio scroll // memra.

(dejecta membra)

when oulippean slips
te *igitur* outrance enters my *ipse dixit*
as sucking
thighs come

in a heuristic cystic vestigial stilled code, a coterie of
hâute calico iliac contours —

                    when houyhnhnmns
                    by whinney out of
                        she-ask

In the simulacrum of a stillness.
In the spectra of sic.iliac echoes.

Which hardens *in me*, in
imminant anamnesis mimesis

of unassimilable (unassimilating) simile
smiles. In the
intimate immensity of
tropophiliac iliac

'cause i fought the shibboleth & the shibboleth fought me.

When uvular fervour fiber spur sequels / In the dissidence of
heresy. In the
passion of interminable secrecy. In
the negligence
of yr feckless exits. or a
curtsey scherzo / in the rhetoric of
the elsewhere. In the
serenity of indifference
abandoned in an idiom

                    i die *in* you.

Entrusted in the limits of the suspect of the

secret of besides.